Ms. Frizzle's Adventures
IMPERIAL CHINA

Ms. Frizzle's Adventures
IMPERIAL CHINA

by JOANNA COLE
illustrated by BRUCE DEGEN

THE ACTION ON A SCROLL MOVES FROM RIGHT TO LEFT.

SCHOLASTIC INC.

NEW YORK TORONTO LONDON AUCKLAND SYDNEY
MEXICO CITY NEW DELHI HONG KONG BUENOS AIRES

For information regarding permission,
write to Scholastic Inc., Attention: Permissions
Department, 557 Broadway, New York, NY 10012.
ISBN-10: 0-439-84328-6 • ISBN-13: 978-0-439-84328-7 • Text
copyright © 2005 by Joanna Cole. Illustrations copyright © 2005 by
Bruce Degen. All rights reserved. Published by Scholastic Inc. SCHOLASTIC,
THE MAGIC SCHOOL BUS, MS. FRIZZLE'S ADVENTURES, and associated logos are
trademarks and/or registered trademarks of Scholastic Inc.
12 11 10 9 8 7 6 5 4 3 2   6 7 8 9 10 11/0   Printed in the U.S.A. 08
First Scholastic Book Club paperback printing, September 2006
The text type was set in 15-point Gill Sans. The illustrator
used brush and ink, pen, and gouache in the artwork.
The author and artist thank Valerie Hansen, Professor
of History at Yale University for her many thoughtful
comments on the manuscript and illustrations;
Kang-i Sun Chang, Professor of Chinese Literature
at Yale University, for her help in finding a suitable
Song dynasty poem; Matthew Towns for his
translation of Su Shi's poem; James Stepanek for
his calligraphy; Phoebe Yeh and Marion Yeh for
their generous comments and insight
from the Chinese American perspective;
and, as always, our heartfelt appreciation
to our editors, Kristin Earhart and Craig
Walker, for their encouragement,
suggestions, and overall wisdom.

To my granddaughter, Annabelle.
May good fortune always
follow her.
—J.C.

To the memory of
Hymie and Mae
and the hot Chinese mustard.
—B.D.

It was the end of the school day,
and I, Ms. Frizzle, was on the move.
Wanda, one of my favorite students,
had invited me to spend
Chinese New Year's Eve with her family.
Wasn't that nice of her?

DRAGON KITE

MAKING KITES

Bamboo Strips

PAPER

FISH KITE

WHERE IS CHINA? CHINA IS IN ASIA

NORTH AMERICA

ASIA

EUROPE

CHINA

AFRICA

SOUTH AMERICA

AUSTRALIA

BUTTERFLY KITE

WHEN IS CHINESE NEW YEAR?

In Western countries, New Year's Day always falls on January 1.

In China, the holiday comes at a different time each year. It can be at the end of January, or in February.

AND IT LASTS FOR 15 WHOLE DAYS!

JANUARY

S	M	Tu	W	Th	F	Sa
	1	2	3	4	5	6
7	8	9	10	11	12	13
14	15	16	17	18	19	20
21	22	23	24	25	26	27
28	29	30	31			

FEBRUARY

S	M	Tu	W	Th	F	Sa
					1	2	3
4	5	6	7	8	9	10
11	12	13	14	15	16	17
18	19	20	21	22	23	24
25	26	27	28			

I had been teaching about China. Now, I was going to celebrate China's most important holiday. It would be fun—and so educational!

LEARNING ABOUT FAR-OFF PLACES IS FUN ISN'T IT, ARNOLD?

FAR-OFF PLACES? UH-OH!

Dear Ms. Frizzle, please come to my house for New Year's Eve dinner. Wanda

FIRST INVENTED IN CHINA

Many things that we use today were invented long ago in ancient China.

KITE-2,400 years ago

That evening, I went to meet Wanda's family. Before dinner, we strolled around Chinatown, taking in the holiday sights.

MEET MY BROTHER, HENRY. I REALLY LOOK UP TO HIM.

PLEASE FORGIVE HENRY'S HAIRSTYLE. HE'S GOING THROUGH A STAGE.

OH, I LOVE IT! IT'S A GREAT LOOK.

FATHER

MOTHER

GRANDMOTHER

◄ THE CHEN FAMILY ►

CHINATOWNS AROUND THE WORLD

In almost every big city, there is an area where many people from China live. Chinese customs are kept alive there.

FIRST INVENTED IN CHINA

UMBRELLA
1,700 years ago

WHAT IT MEANS IN CHINA

Chinese bride

The COLOR RED means happiness and good luck.

We were walking on a busy street
when we had a big surprise.
Arnold, another one of my favorite students,
was getting dropped off for his kung fu class.
Of course, he was very glad to see us.

9

The New Year's festival was exciting.
A cloth dragon came winding down the street.
Men were under the dragon, making it dance.
Wanda has always been an adventurous girl,
but even I was surprised by what she did next.

YOU CAN'T GO UNDER THERE—YOU'LL MISS DINNER!

I CAN'T GO UNDER HERE—I'LL MISS KUNG FU!

WHAT IT MEANS IN CHINA

The Dragon means good luck and power. It was a symbol of the Emperor in ancient China.

Dragon painting

Dragon pottery

Dragon robe

Wanda ducked under the dragon.
Henry followed her, and naturally,
Arnold was eager to join them.
I, Ms. Frizzle, went too.
After all, someone had to make sure
they didn't get too far from home.

IT'S COOL, ARNIE.
YOU CAN TAKE A
MAKEUP CLASS.

We were under the dragon
for a long time.

When the dragon came to a stop, we peeked out. Chinatown was gone! We were in a farmers' village in China, and it was one thousand years ago! I had plenty of Chinese clothing in my bag, so we fit right in. The villagers were just ending their fifteen-day New Year's celebration.

The New Year celebration ends with the beautiful Lantern Festival. The children carry lanterns all around the village.

Even though we were complete strangers, the farmers shared their food with us and invited us to stay overnight.

HOW TO USE CHOPSTICKS

1. Hold chopstick like a pencil.

2. Lift away thumb and index finger.

3. Now the bottom stick rests between the thumb and ring finger. Hold top chopstick like a pencil.

4. To pick up food, move the top chopstick. The bottom stick always stays still.

The next morning, we helped the farmers work in the rice fields. Arnold wanted to learn all about growing rice.

RICE LIKES TO GROW IN WATER...

AND IT LIKES WARM PLACES...

JUST LIKE HERE— NEAR THE RIVER.

RIVER

HOW TO GROW RICE

1. Flood rice fields with a few inches of water.

CHAIN PUMP

2. Plow fields.

SIMPLE PLOW

WATER BUFFALO

3. Plant seedlings by hand.

As we worked, we talked with our new friends.
They had a very hard life, and it had not
been a good year for farming.
This year, their rice crop was small.

WE'LL HAVE LESS RICE TO SELL.

WE MAY GO HUNGRY.

THINGS WILL BE HARD FOR US.

YOUR WATER BUFFALO IS MAKING THINGS HARD FOR ME!

BONK

STAY COOL, ARNIE! I AM!

4. Weed fields by hand until rice is ready.

5. Drain fields and harvest rice.

6. Beat grains from stalks. (This is called threshing.)

Farmers' families had to sell lots of rice to earn enough money to pay their taxes. When the rice crop was small, the governor was supposed to make the taxes lower, but this year he wanted to keep the same high taxes.

WE CAN'T PAY OUR TAXES.

THE EMPEROR MIGHT HELP US. EVERYONE KNOWS HE IS KIND.

BUT THE EMPEROR IS FAR AWAY.

PAY ATTENTION TO THIS WORD

When you pay <u>TAXES</u>, you give some of what you earn to the government.

WE USE YOUR MONEY FOR ROADS, CANALS, ARMIES...

...PALACES, JEWELS, FANCY CLOTHES FOR THE GOVERNOR.

COLLECT THE TAXES NOW!

| Tax collector | Farmer | Tax collector | THE GOVERNOR |

The great Yangtze River flowed past the farm.
That gave Wanda an idea.
"Let's go talk to the Emperor about this," she said.
I, Ms. Frizzle, did not hesitate.
Right then and there, I booked us passage
on a river barge headed for the palace.

ALL THE CHINESE GOVERNORS HAVE TO OBEY ME!

THE EMPEROR

STAY COOL, FARM PEOPLE. WE'LL GO ASK THE EMPEROR FOR HELP.

BUT EMPERORS NEVER TALK TO ORDINARY PEOPLE.

THEY DON'T LOOK ORDINARY TO ME.

THE RIVER DELIVERS

Barges carried rice to sell in the northern parts of China. Barges were pulled by men or animals.

We cruised down the river, eating, drinking tea,
and sleeping on board.
We stopped along the way to pick up more loads of rice.
Finally, we came to the Grand Canal, which
would take us north to the Emperor.
There, a new traveler came aboard.

FIRST BREWED IN CHINA

TEA~ 2,300 Years ago
People around the world
drink tea more than
any other beverage
except water.

1. Tips of tea bushes
are picked.

2. Tea leaves are
dried and prepared.

3. Tea is
brewed
with hot
water
in teapots.

4. In ancient China tea
was often sipped
from bowls
instead of cups.

Our new passenger was a poet named Su Shi.
As soon as he came on the boat,
he started to write a poem.
I, Ms. Frizzle, was delighted!
I even copied it in English for my class's China studies.

IN ANCIENT CHINA, PEOPLE WROTE WITH INK AND A BRUSH.

CAN'T SOMEONE LEND HIM A BALLPOINT PEN?

SORRY, ARNOLD! NOT IN THIS CENTURY.

chinese writing reads from top to bottom, and from right to left.

橫看成嶺側成峰
遠近高低各不同
不識盧山真面目
只緣身在此山中

POEM IN ENGLISH
From the side,
    a whole range,
From the end,
    a single peak.
Far, near, high, low,
    no two parts alike.
Why can't I tell the
    true shape
        of Mt. Lu?
Because I myself
    am in the mountain.

CHINESE WRITING

Chinese writers use symbols called "characters." Each one stands for a word. Combining two characters can make another word.

火山
Fire + Mountain = Volcano

There were special supplies for writing and drawing in ancient China:

Inkstick   Inkstone   Water Jar   Bamboo Brushes

To make Chinese ink, rub an inkstick with water on an inkstone until the ink in the well is as dark as you wish.

Inkstick
Well
Inkstone

In his travels, the poet had learned that the Emperor would be leaving the capital soon. There were many rich palaces in China, and the Emperor lived in them, one after another. Oh, dear! We had to get to the capital fast, or we would miss the Emperor!

THE EMPEROR WILL GO AWAY VERY SOON.

WON'T THIS BOAT GO FASTER?

I DON'T THINK SO...

FIRST INVENTED IN CHINA

RUDDER
for steering a boat
2,000 years ago

Rudder

COMPASS
for finding direction
more than 1,000 years ago

Magnetized needle

Float

Bowl of water

Simple Mariner's Compass

As we came up to a bridge, another barge drifted in front of us.
Crunch! Both barges were damaged.
We had to abandon ship.
Even I, Ms. Frizzle, didn't know how we'd ever get to the capital soon enough!

We found ourselves in a busy town,
and there was so much to see!
We were buying some souvenirs, when
we were invited to learn how silk is made.
Somehow, we just couldn't say no.

COME WITH US.

WE NEED WORKERS.

FIRST INVENTED IN CHINA

PAPER
about 2,100 years ago
Paper was made by grinding mulberry bark
into pulp and spreading it on a screen to dry
into sheets.

PAPER MONEY
about 1,000 years ago
Before paper money, chinese coins were
made of bronze. They had square holes
for stringing.

THIS MONEY IS
TOO HEAVY!

TRY SOME
OF THIS!

SILK
MORE THAN 4,000 YEARS AGO

For hundreds of years, no one knew how to make silk except the Chinese. After a while, the secret was smuggled to other countries.

At the factory, we started learning
the silk trade right away.
Making silk is hard work.
Now, I usually do not mind hard work,
but we were on a mission.
We had to get to the capital city and
talk to the Emperor!

MULBERRY TREES

WE HAVE TO
GET AWAY!

IT WON'T
BE EASY.

HOW TO MAKE SILK

1. Feed silkworms. (They eat
only mulberry leaves.)

2. Let worms spin cocoons
out of silk.

ACTUAL SIZE

3. Dip cocoons in hot water
to dissolve sticky stuff.

THIS ISN'T COOL.

IT'S HOT!

Finally, Arnold found a clever way to escape. He showed us how to stow away in a cart that was carrying silk north.

4. Unwind silk fibers.

5. Spin the thin fibers into thicker threads.

6. Dye threads.

7. Weave them into beautiful silk cloth.

As we went farther north, the climate became drier and cooler. It wasn't good for growing rice. Instead, farmers grew wheat here. After a while, the bumping of the cart lulled us to sleep.

FOOD FOR THOUGHT

THE SOUTH WAS NICE FOR RICE.

THE NORTH WAS NEAT FOR WHEAT.

Rice

Rice noodles

Wheat buns

Wheat noodles

Wheat dumplings

OUR JOURNEY SO FAR

The Great Wall

We are here.

The Grand Canal

We started here.

Wheat region
Rice region

When we woke up,
we had gone too far.
We had missed the capital.
We had come all the way
to the Great Wall of China!
The wall was built to keep
out invaders, and at that
very moment, an invading
army was trying to get in.

THE GREAT WALL:
1,000 YEARS AGO
At first it was made of
mounds of earth with spaces
in between. Sometimes it fell
down and had to be rebuilt.

THE GREAT WALL:
TODAY
It finally became a stone wall
3,000 miles long. It is the
largest human-made
structure on Earth.

IT TOOK THOUSANDS OF YEARS...

...AND MILLIONS OF WORKERS...

...TO BUILD THIS WALL.

Warriors from lands to the north were fighting on horseback. They wanted to conquer and rule China. The Chinese soldiers were fighting back from the top of the dirt wall.

TAKE THAT!

AARRGGHH!

FIRST INVENTED IN CHINA

CROSSBOW
2,300 years ago

A crossbow was faster and more powerful than an ordinary bow and arrow.

GUNPOWDER
1,200 years ago

Arrows could now carry gunpowder charges.

STEEL
1,500 years ago

Swords could be made of steel.

Finally, we came to the capital city and found the Emperor's beautiful palace. The guards had strict orders to keep us out. They also had very sharp weapons.

WE NEED SOME SWORD PRACTICE.

WHY NOT PRACTICE ON THESE STRANGERS?

STRANGE IS RIGHT! I'LL GO FIRST.

CHINA'S CHANGING CAPITAL

China's capital has moved many times. In the 11th century it was Kaifeng.

Today the capital is Beijing. This city has been the capital several times over thousands of years.

In Beijing you can still visit the ancient Emperor's palace in a walled area called the Forbidden City.

THE FORBIDDEN CITY

It looked like they were going to use their swords on us. Fortunately, they changed their minds. We just had to get inside the palace and find the Emperor.

We entered the palace, passing beautiful furniture, jade sculptures, and porcelain vases. Treasures were all around us, but the person we were looking for was nowhere to be seen. Was he even in the palace? We hoped we weren't too late!

FIRST INVENTED IN CHINA

PORCELAIN
about 1,500 years ago
Pottery is clay fired in an oven.
Porcelain is a very, very fine quality of pottery that is used to make vases and dishes.
Because porcelain was first invented in China, English-speaking people call all dishes "china."

EARTHQUAKE DETECTOR
about 1,500 years ago
When the earth shakes, metal balls fall into the mouths of the toads, and show the direction and strength of the quake.

Then Wanda, who was always running ahead, looked in a doorway and made a grand discovery. Thank goodness—the Emperor of China was still at home!

LOOK, MS. FRIZZLE! I FOUND HIM!

COOL OUTFIT, EMP!

CAN WE GET HIS AUTOGRAPH?

BE RESPECTFUL, KIDS.

JADE CARVING
5,000 years ago
Jade is a rare stone that is carved into jewelry and statues.

PIN   DISC   JAR

WHAT IT MEANS IN CHINA

IMPERIAL YELLOW
The Emperor's robes were a special shade of yellow. Nobody but the Emperor was allowed to wear that color.

The Emperor was not only the ruler of a great country, he was a talented artist, too.
He turned from his painting and asked what we wanted.
Wanda told him all about the farmers' village, the small rice crop, and the unfair taxes.
I, Ms. Frizzle, was so proud of her!

PLEASE SAVE THE VILLAGERS, YOUR MAJESTY. WITHOUT YOUR HELP, THE FARMERS' FAMILIES WILL GO HUNGRY.

DON'T YOU KNOW HOW TO BOW, LITTLE GIRL?

HOW TO BOW IN ANCIENT CHINA

Kneel three times.
For each kneel, touch your forehead to the floor three times.
This bow is called ketou or, in English, kowtow...

KOWTOW?

OW!

ONE, TWO, THREE...

The Emperor understood at once.
He announced that there would be no taxes
that year for farmers who had small rice crops!
He sent an official to inform the village's governor.

Now it was time to leave.

YIKES! YET ANOTHER GUARD, AND HE'S AFTER US!

STAY COOL, ARNIE!

THIS IS NO TIME TO BE COOL, HENRY!

We knew we had to get home. Unfortunately, the guard was in our way. Fortunately, Arnold had some fast moves.

HAI-AH!

YIKES! HE KNOWS KUNG FU!

LOOK, MS. FRIZZLE! ARNOLD IS PRACTICING HIS KUNG FU!

HIS MOTHER WILL BE SO PLEASED.

QUICK! LET'S GET OUT OF HERE!

FIRST INVENTED IN CHINA

KUNG FU ~ Thousands of years ago
Kung fu is a kind of unarmed martial art.
UNARMED - without weapons
MARTIAL - fighting
ART - skill

WHAT IT MEANS IN CHINA

The lion is thought to guard against danger. Lion sculptures are often put outside a door. It is good luck to rub a paw as you go by.

Our luck continued.
Wanda came upon a handy door.
It was an amazing door.
In fact, it was the door to . . .

FIRST SET OFF IN CHINA
FIREWORKS—3,000 years ago
used for celebrations

...Wanda and Henry's dining room!
Everyone was waiting for us,
and dinner was on the table.
There were many foods that stood for
good things to come in the New Year.

WHERE WERE YOU?

WE WERE SO WORRIED!

SOUP —
everything better
than last year

TANGERINES —
good fortune

APPLES —
peace

SWEET RICE CAKE —
more wealth every year

FISH ~ plenty

CHICKEN ~ wealth
in the New Year

MUSTARD GREENS —
a green year for farmers